WNF
29.93
12/17

EELS

Darla Duhaime

Rourke Educational Media

rourkeeducationalmedia.com

Before & After Reading Activities

Teaching Focus:
Concepts of Print- Have students find capital letters and punctuation in a sentence. Ask students to explain the purpose for using them in a sentence.

Before Reading:

Building Academic Vocabulary and Background Knowledge
Before reading a book, it is important to set the stage for your child or student by using pre-reading strategies. This will help them develop their vocabulary, increase their reading comprehension, and make connections across the curriculum.
1. *Read the title and look at the cover. Let's make predictions about what this book will be about.*
2. *Take a picture walk by talking about the pictures/photographs in the book. Implant the vocabulary as you take the picture walk. Be sure to talk about the text features such as headings, Table of Contents, glossary, bolded words, captions, charts/diagrams, or Index.*
3. Have students read the first page of text with you then have students read the remaining text.
4. *Strategy Talk – use to assist students while reading.*
   - *Get your mouth ready*
   - *Look at the picture*
   - *Think…does it make sense*
   - *Think…does it look right*
   - *Think…does it sound right*
   - *Chunk it – by looking for a part you know*
5. *Read it again.*

Content Area Vocabulary
Use glossary words in a sentence.

marine
nocturnal
predators
prey

After Reading:

Comprehension and Extension Activity
After reading the book, work on the following questions with your child or students in order to check their level of reading comprehension and content mastery.
1. *How does an eel find its prey? (Summarize)*
2. *What are gills? (Asking Questions)*
3. *Would you eat an eel? (Text to Self Connection)*
4. *How many species of eels are there in the world? (Asking Questions)*

Extension Activity
Find a long, old sock. The longer, the better! Stuff the sock with tissue or other soft paper until it is completely full. Use a rubber band to close the opening after it is stuffed. Add eyes and a mouth using markers, buttons, or other found objects. Now you have your own stuffed eel. What will you name it?

Table of Contents

Marine Eels   4
Hiding and Hunting   10
Baby Eels   18
Fun Facts   22
Picture Glossary   23
Index   24
Websites to Visit   24
About the Author   24

Marine Eels

Marine eels live in salty oceans and seas. They look like snakes. But they are not snakes. They are fish!

Like other fish, eels have fins and gills. Eels breathe through their gills. Their fins help them swim.

Eels can swim forward and backward. Some can travel on land!

Hiding and Hunting

Most eels are **nocturnal**. They rest during the day and hunt at night.

Eels are **predators**. They burrow in sand. They hide among reefs and rocks. They wait for **prey** to swim near.

Eels can't see or hear well. They have a strong sense of smell to find food.

Eels have sharp teeth. They eat fish, octopuses, crabs, mollusks, and squid.

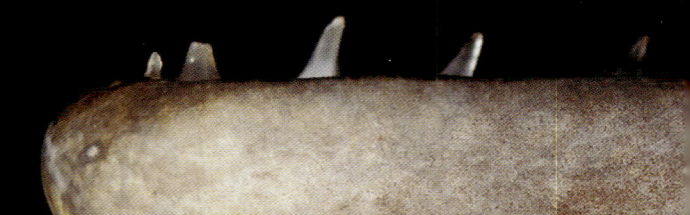

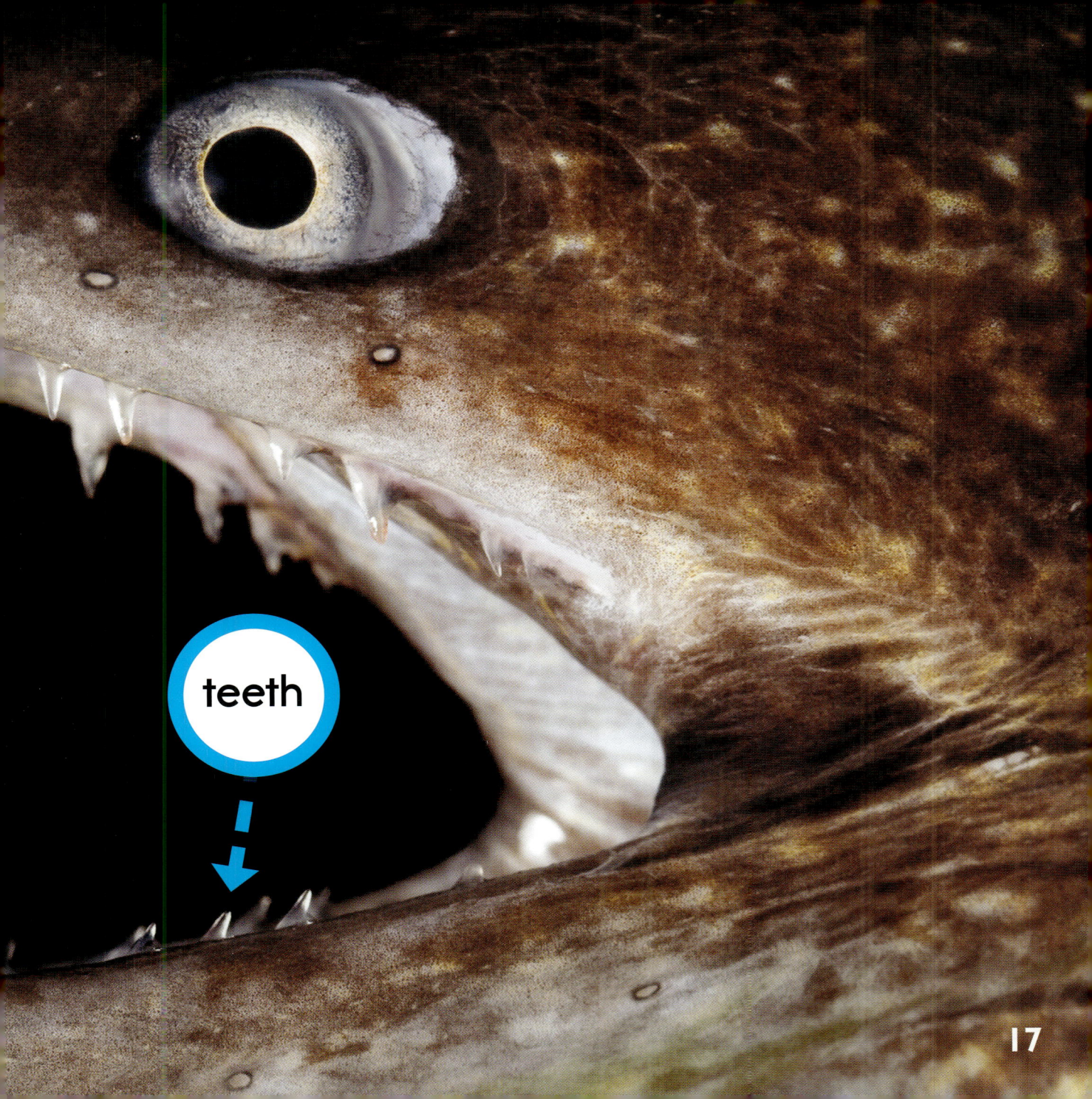

Baby Eels

Some eels travel up to 4,000 miles (6,437 kilometers) to breed. They lay their eggs in the open ocean.

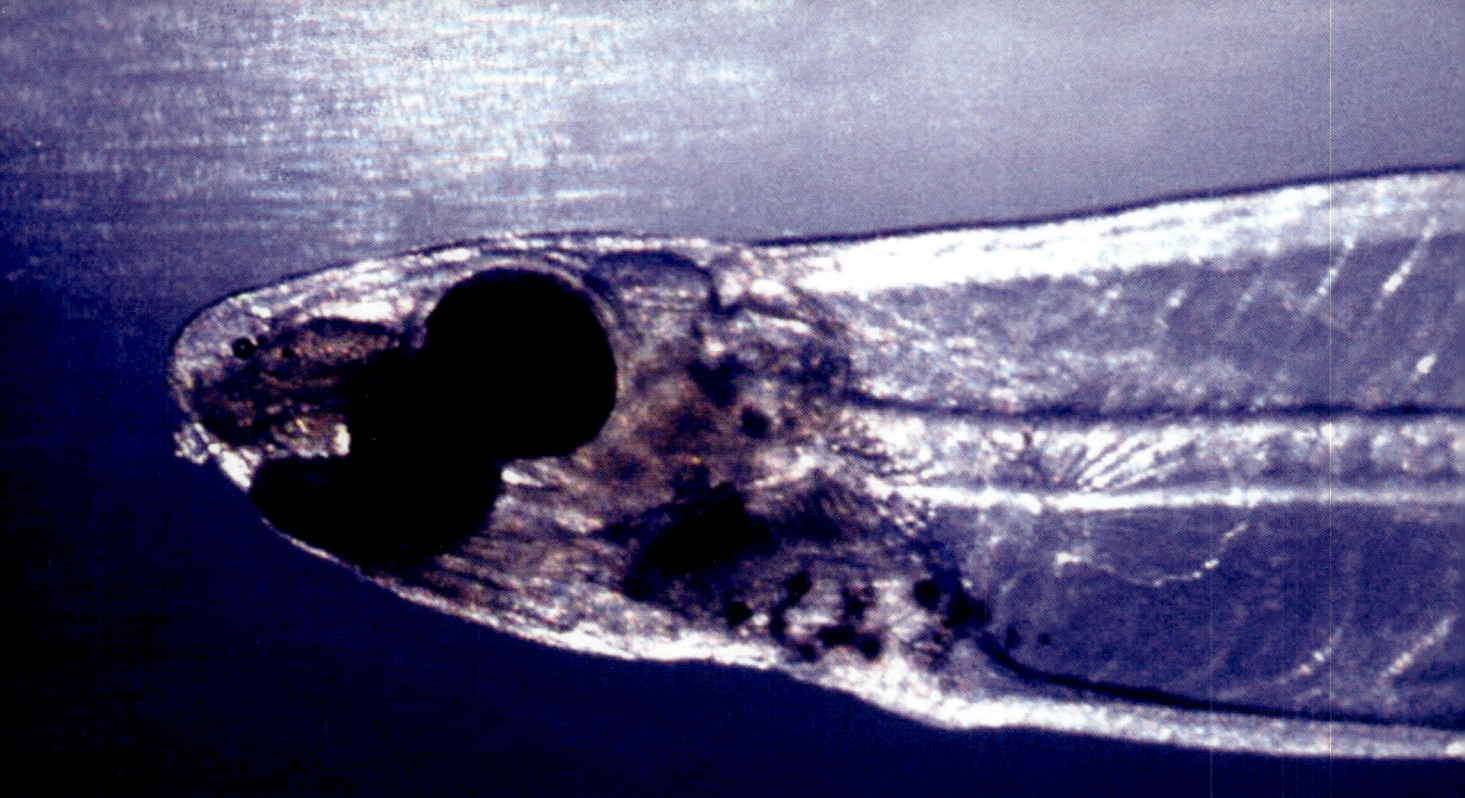

Larvae hatch from the eggs. The larvae float in the water. You can see right through them!

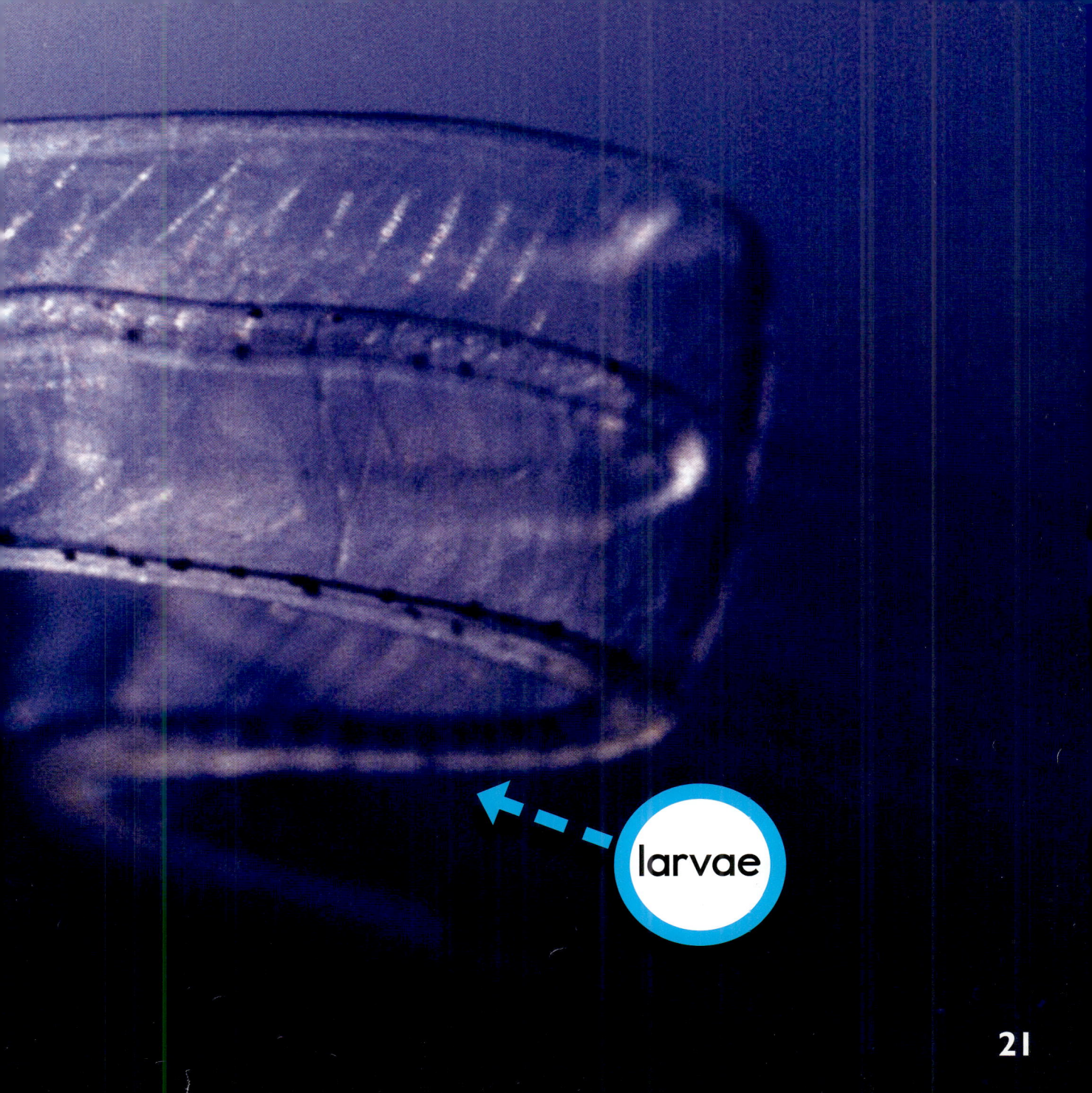

Fun Facts

- It takes about three years for an eel to become an adult.

- An eel's backbone has more than 100 vertebrae.

- There are more than 800 species of eels in the world.

- European congers are the largest eel species. They can weigh up to 240 pounds (110 kilograms).

Picture Glossary

marine (muh-REEN): Living in or part of an ocean or sea.

nocturnal (nahk-TUR-nuhl): A nocturnal animal is active at night.

predators (PRED-uh-turs): Animals that hunt other animals for food.

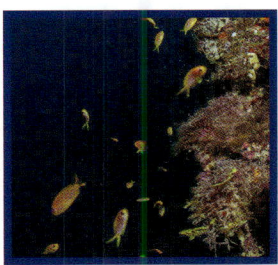

prey (pray): An animal that is hunted by another animal for food.

Index

fin(s) 6, 7
gills 6, 7
larvae 20, 21
swim 6, 8, 12
teeth 16, 17

Websites to Visit

www.fws.gov/northeast/newsroom/facts.html
study.com/academy/lesson/moray-eel-facts-lesson-for-kids.html
www.keywestaquarium.com/eels

Meet The Author!
www.meetREMauthors.com

About the Author

Darla Duhaime is fascinated by sea creatures and their amazing ocean habitats. When she is not writing books for kids, you can often find her gazing at the ocean, dreaming up new stories.

© 2018 Rourke Educational Media

All rights reserved. No part of this book may be reproduced or utilized in any form or by any means, electronic or mechanical including photocopying, recording, or by any information storage and retrieval system without permission in writing from the publisher.

www.rourkeeducationalmedia.com

PHOTO CREDITS: Cover and title page: ©blickwinkel/Alamy Stock Photo; p.5, 23: ©Pavel Vakhrushev; p.7: ©dsafanda; p.9: ©graham melling; p.11, 23: ©scubaluna; p.13, 23: ©Rostislavv; p.15, 23: ©Supermaw; p.16-17: ©miljko; p.19: ©ND; p20-21: Wikipedia

Edited by: Keli Sipperley
Cover and Interior design by: Rhea Magaro-Wallace

Library of Congress PCN Data

Eels / Darla Duhaime
(Ocean Animals)
ISBN (hard cover)(alk. paper) 978-1-68342-325-6
ISBN (soft cover) 978-1-68342-421-5
ISBN (e-Book) 978-1-68342-491-8
Library of Congress Control Number: 2017931172

Printed in the United States of America, North Mankato, Minnesota